Make Money Online In Cryptocurrency

Mastering Hive Publishing for Web3 Wealth in 2024

By

Ray J Corbett

Table of Contents

Introduction

Something fresh has developed in an era characterized by rapid innovation, one that has the potential to fundamentally alter the internet and our connection with it. Greetings from Web3, a paradigm change that surpasses the constraints of its predecessors.

The notion of Web3 signifies a basic advancement beyond the well-known terrain of Web1 and Web2. Web3 emerges as a decentralized, trustless, and more democratized version of the internet, whereas Web1 introduced us to the World Wide Web with static web pages and inadequate interactivity, and Web2 transformed connectivity and interaction with others through platforms like social media and user-generated content.

Fundamentally, Web3 transforms how we interact with the internet. Transparency, decentralization, and cryptographic security are the pillars around which this decentralized ecosystem is constructed. Blockchain technology is the foundation of Web3, enabling peer-to-peer exchanges and transactions eliminating the need for middlemen. By giving people more control over their data, identities, and digital assets, this empowers individuals.

Hive, a cutting-edge decentralized platform that reintroduce content production and delivery, is a major participant in the Web3 scene. As an example of the potential of Web3, Hive provides a decentralized, community-driven platform for creative people to publish, interact, and make money.

This book takes us on a deep dive into Web3, with a particular emphasis on learning Hive as a means of not just surviving but thriving in this new digital age. In order to help you get around the decentralized landscape, take advantage of its opportunities, and discover the potential for wealth creation in 2024 and beyond, this guide aims to demystify Web3, whether you're a content creator, a writer, an entrepreneur, or you're just curious about the abilities of this transformative technology. Greetings from the internet's future.

Overview of Hive: A Platform for Decentralized Publishing

Within Web3, where decentralization and empowerment are the ruler, Hive is a shining example of innovation that is changing the face of content distribution and production.

Comprehending the Foundation of Hive

- **Decentralization Fundamentals**: As a decentralized, community-driven network, Hive is based on the ideas of broadening participation, transparency, and individuality. Because of its blockchain-based operation, it promotes a trustless environment in which users and content producers have total control over their interactions and data.

- **Blockchain Structure**: Hive guarantees a scalable and effective network where users may create, share, and interact without the limitations of conventional centralized platforms by employing a delegated proof-of-stake (DPoS) consensus process.

Revealing the Special Qualities of Hive

- **Tokenized Rewards**: Hive creates a lively ecosystem where users are rewarded for their significant involvement by rewarding content authors and curators with cryptocurrency (Hive tokens) depending on the caliber and engagement of their contributions.
- **Decentralized Governance**: Hive's governance style gives its community the ability to take part in decision-making processes, influencing the course, innovations, and enhancements of the platform.

- **Diversified Ecosystem of Communities**: Hive supports a variety of groups, referred to as "Hive tribes," each with their own specialization, passions, and customs. This fosters the growth of specialized markets for creators and fans.

How to Get Around the Hive Experience

- **Producing and Disseminating Content**: Discover how to publish content quickly and easily using Hive's user-friendly interface. Content producers may easily share their stories and knowledge through blog entries and multimedia material.

Hive fosters a culture of connection and appreciation for outstanding content by encouraging active participation through upvotes and comments. This approach combines engagement with curation. Users also have the ability to select and honor information that they believe is notable.

- **Earning and Monetization**: Users may earn Hive tokens, which allow for direct platform monetization, by participating in the community and producing high-quality content.

Embracing the Future with Hive

Hive continues to be at the vanguard of the Web3 scene, demonstrating the promise for decentralized, rewarding, and censorship-resistant content platforms. It is a key participant in determining how digital content is shaped going forward because of its dedication to enabling both creators and users.

Hive is an invitation to investigate a new age of content production and distribution one in which the community has the power because of its decentralized structure, open governance, and creative incentives.

Other Platforms under the Hive Blockchain

As a blockchain ecosystem, Hive is home to several communities and platforms, each serving a distinct set of needs and interests. Here is a summary of a few well-known Hive blockchain platforms:

1. Hive.blog

Link: https://hive.blog

Description: Hive.blog is the main platform for Hive user interaction and content development. It provides an easy-to-use blogging platform where content producers may post articles, publish multimedia files, and interact with readers by leaving comments and giving each other votes.

2. PeakD

Link: https://peakd.com

Description: PeakD is a feature-rich front-end interface for Hive that provides an improved social media, community participation, and content production user experience. It offers consumers customized feed choices, portfolio tracking, and sophisticated analytics.

3. 3Speak

Link: https://3speak.tv

Description: 3Speak is a decentralized video-sharing platform on Hive that gives content producers the freedom to distribute a wide range of content, without any restrictions. It places a strong emphasis on free expression and seeks to offer an alternative to popular video hosting services.

4. D.Buzz

link: https://d.buzz

Description: D.Buzz is a microblogging platform available on Hive that facilitates the rapid and interesting sharing of short-form contents, updates, and opinions by users. It promotes community engagement and succinct storytelling.

5. Ecency

Link : https://ecency.com

Description: With its options for social engagement, content production, and curation, Ecency is a flexible front-end interface that improves the Hive experience. It highlights a smooth and intuitive user experience for users of Hive.

6. LeoFinance

Link: https://leofinance.io

Description: LeoFinance is a specialized forum for debates, insights, and analysis about blockchain, cryptocurrencies, and financial markets. It concentrates on finance and cryptocurrency-related contents.

7. Splinterlands

Link: www.splinterlands.com

Description: Developed on the Hive blockchain, Splinterlands is a well-known digital collectible card game based on blockchain technology. With digital cards, players may duel, trade, and collect while earning rewards in bitcoin.

8. The STEMGeeks

Link: https://stemgeeks.net/

Description: The goal of STEMGeeks is to create and host information related to science, technology, engineering, and mathematics (STEM). It promotes information and insight exchange in STEM-related domains.

These platforms, which provide a variety of specialized places for producers and enthusiasts, highlight the Hive blockchain's adaptability and diversity. Every platform adds to the dynamic ecosystem on the Hive blockchain with its own distinct features, communities, and goals.

Chapter 2: Getting Started with Hive

Setting up Your Hive Account

Choose your preferred front-end interface before establishing your account. Hive has a variety of interfaces, each with an own set of functionality and user experience, such as Hive.blog, PeakD, or Ecency.

Go to the interface of your choice to begin the registration process.

I'll be creating a new account for the purposes of this lesson, I will utilize Leofinance platform and Ecency for clarity.

Steps to set up your account:

1. Go to https://hive.blog on your browser, click on sign up.

Figure 1: Source- Hive.blog

2. Scroll down to select any of the registration providers.

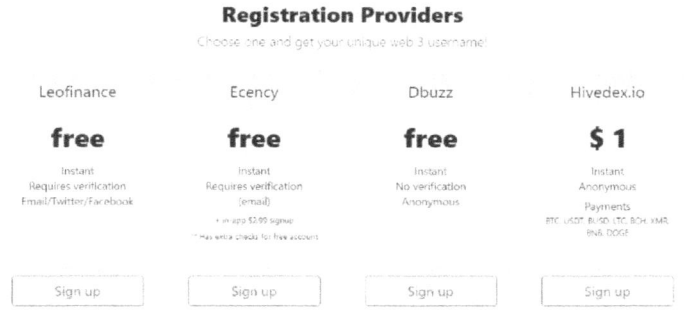

Figure2: Source- Hive.Blog

I'll be walking you through the process of signing up with Leofinance and ecency for the sake of this tutorial. All you need to do is select and register with a single provider.

If using Leofinance

3. Click the Signup button beneath Leofinance to begin the registration process.

Make sure your Facebook, Twitter, and email accounts are all active.

4. As can be seen below, click the signup button on the right side of the screen.

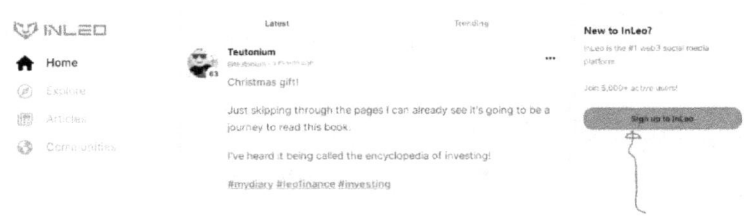

Figure 3: Source- leofinance.io

5. Select create a hive account as seen below.

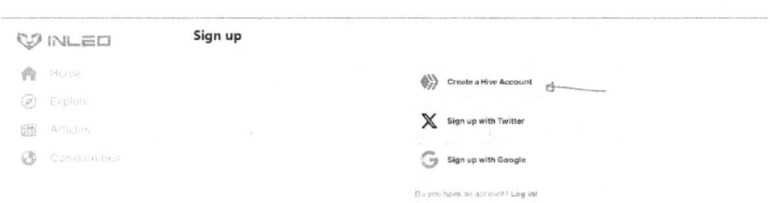

Figure 4: Source- leofinance.io

Kindly read through the information displayed as seen below before you click on continue.

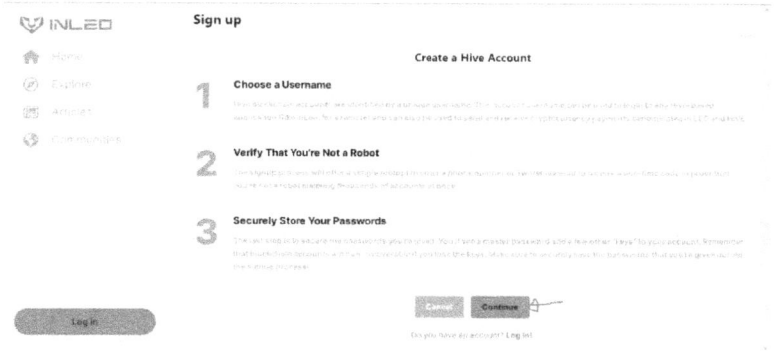

Figure 5: Source-leofinance.io

6. Enter your preferred username, select a verification method and click on download keys.

Figure 6: Source--leofinance.io

The download of your keys will happen automatically. Press the "continue" button.

After successfully connecting your Twitter account, you will receive a congratulations message for your successful signup.

If using Ecency

If you choose Ecency registration, follow the steps below.

1. Select Ecency as your registration provider.
2. Click on signup.
3. Enter your username and email address and select continue.

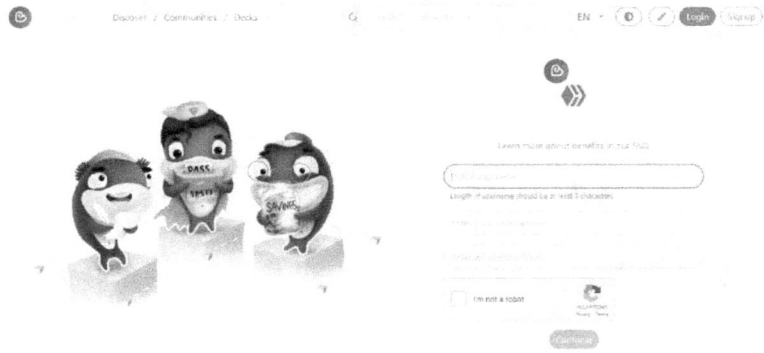

Figure 7: Source--ecency.com

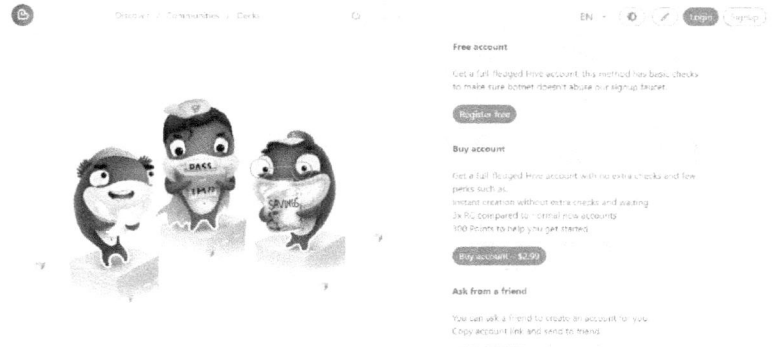

Figure 8: Source--ecency.com

4. Click on register free.

As instructed, download your keys.

If a "IP quality is low" prompt appears, consider using a different network or a different time frame.

Note that a request to download your keys will appear.

Understanding Hive Keys

Following a successful registration process, a file containing your log-in keys will need to be downloaded. Make sure you keep these keys offline in a secure location.

Included with the keys are the following:

- **Username**: the username that you registered under.
- **Active Private Key**: The active private key is utilized for a number of account-related operations, including posting, voting, and money transfers.
- **Active Public Key**: The public key that corresponds to the active private key is called the active public key. It is employed to confirm operations carried out using the Active Private Key.
- **Posting Private Key**: The main use of this key on the site is to publish comments and content.

- **Posting Public Key**: Verifying posts and comments made using the Posting Private Key requires the Posting Public Key, which is the public key that corresponds to it.
- **Owner Private Key**: With this key, you may change any other key, retrieve the account, and modify permissions, giving you complete access and control over the account. This key is the strongest one connected to the account.
- **Owner Public Key**: This is the public key that matches the Owner Private Key and is used to authenticate transactions made using the Owner Private Key.
- **Memo Key**: This key is only used to encrypt and decode transaction notes, giving users a safe means to exchange private messages via the blockchain.
- **Master Password**: It's possible that this password is used to control and access these keys. Because this password provides access to the account's keys, it must be kept private.

Examining the Features and Interface of Hive

You need to log into your account with your username and posting private key in order to explore the Hive interface.

The hive platform is easy to use; you may use the same log-in credentials to explore the other hive platforms that were mentioned previously.

Log into your account

1. Visit https://hive.blog

Sign in with your username and posting private key. You will be welcomed by the interface below.

Figure 9: Source--hive.blog

Quickly set your account by updating your profile.

2. Click on the human icon on your right screen, select profile.

Figure 10: Source--hive.blog

3. On the right side of the screen where you find setting, click on it.

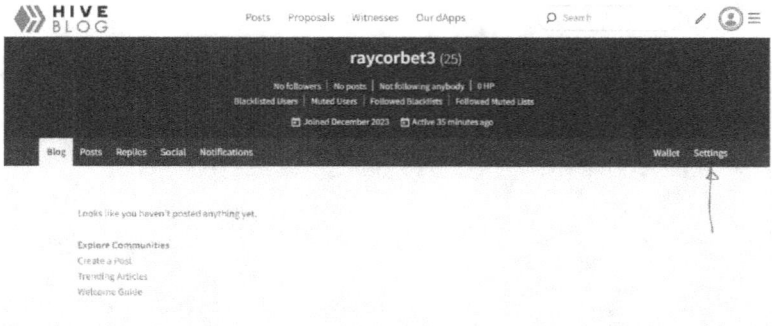

Figure 11: Source - hive.blog

4. Upload your profile picture, cover image, display name, about-you-self, if you have a website, also indicate as well.

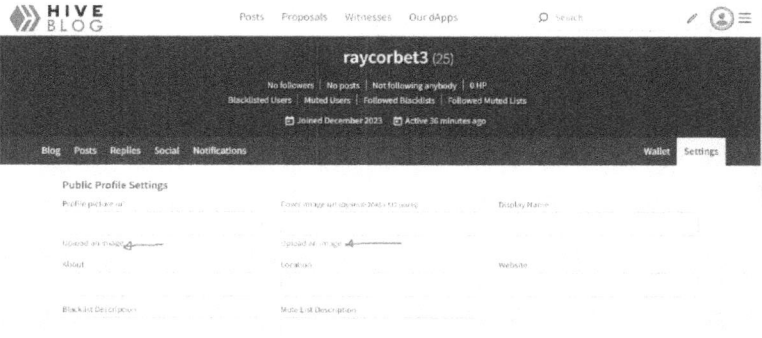

Figure 12: Source -hive.blog

Hive Wallet: You may manage your digital assets, like HIVE tokens and other platform-related tokens, in your Hive wallet.

All you need is your login and active private key to access your Hive wallet. Log into your wallet to get your benefits if you receive payment for a post that you own after seven days after its publication.

The "Notification" tab:

This tab contains all of your received alerts. Every time you use the blockchain, be sure to constantly check the tab. additionally, reply and interact with the subject matter as well.

The "Social" tab

To choose and browse content from the users you follow on the platform, navigate to the "Social" option on the Hive interface. You may interact with posts, debates, and comments from people you're connected with.

The "Replies" tab

The Hive interface's "Replies" page is a component that compiles all of the interactions and answers that are explicitly addressed to you. Direct Answers are among them. It compiles feedback and direct responses from other users to your posts or comments. This enables you to monitor discussions about your content.

Notifications of mentions in posts and comments that include your username (before the "@" sign) will also show up in the "Replies" page.

The "Post" tab

The portion of the Hive interface where you may create, manage, and see your own posts is commonly referred to as the "Post" tab.

The "Blog" tab

Similar to a personal blog or feed, the "Blog" tab on the Hive interface usually acts as a focal spot where users may display their own published content in order of publication.

These are some additional elements of the hive interface, listed below.

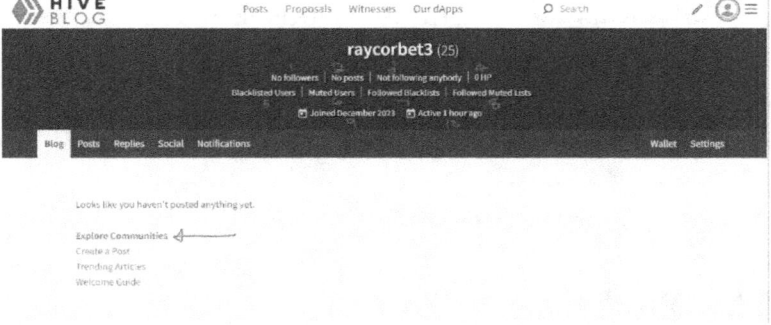

Figure 13: Source --hive.blog

Here is a breakdown of the numbering:

1: denotes users who are following you on the network.

2: is a representation of how many posts, including comments, you have made on the platform.

3: is a representation of the quantity of followers you have.

Following users on the site is crucial if you want to view their posts as soon as they are published and become used to the posting guidelines.

4: stands for your hive strength, or influence, on the blockchain. What you should know about possessing hive power is as follows.

Within the Hive blockchain ecosystem, a user's influence, stake, and dedication are measured using Hive Power (HP). In essence, it shows the degree of a user's vested impact on the site.

This is how Hive Power is broken down:

- **Stake in the Platform**: The vested interest of a user in the Hive blockchain is represented by Hive Power. By exchanging their liquid HIVE tokens for Hive Power, users may obtain Hive Power. This procedure, known as "Powering Up," is a means of demonstrating one's dedication to the platform.

- **Governance and impact**: A user's impact on the platform is based on how much Hive Power they possess. Higher Hive Power users can vote for witnesses (block producers), curate content through upvotes, and participate in governance initiatives, among other platform choices.

- **Long-Term Devotion**: Unlike standard HIVE tokens, Hive Power is difficult to sell. It needs to go through a procedure known as "Powering Down," which takes a while (about 13 weeks) to gradually convert Hive Power back into liquid HIVE tokens. Long-term dedication is encouraged by this architecture, which also lessens volatility brought on by abrupt, significant sell-offs.

- **Enhanced Capabilities:** Gaining more Hive Power grants access to new features and functionalities on the platform. Higher Hive Power members, for instance, may receive greater curation rewards, which increases their desire to upvote and curate material.

5: depicts Blacklisted users - Users who wish to exclude particular accounts from engaging with them or their material may do so by using the "Blacklisted Users" tab on Hive as a management tool.

6: muted users: Hive's "Muted Users" feature lets users manage how they connect with other users by muting particular accounts. A user can choose to restrict their exposure to another account's conversations or material without fully banning them by muting that account.

For a beginner, other features like 7, 8 might not be significant.

9: is a representation of the year and month you joined Hive.

10: denotes the last active session.

Getting Involved In Communities Related To Your Passion

Joining groups on Hive that align with your interests is crucial to beginning your publishing career and supporting a variety of interests.

Additionally, it's a good idea to get involved with a community with a sizable subscriber base that aligns with your interests in order to meet like-minded individuals.

To join communities on Hive:

Select the "blog" tab and click on "explore communities" to join a community.

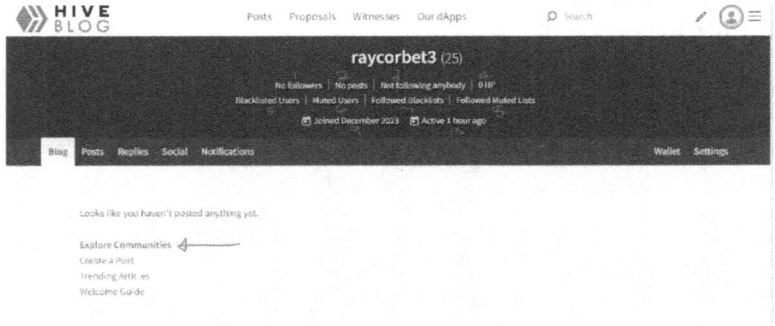

Figure 14: Source --hive.blog

Carefully read through the type of activity each communities on hive supports.

Remember to hit the "subscribe" button, if any suits your passion.

Figure 15: Source--hive.blog

As long as the community supports the posts you make there, you are free to join as many communities as you like on Hive.

On Hive, inappropriate conduct will not be accepted, such as publishing the incorrect article in communities that don't support it.

For example, posting about a clothing you made in a group called Leofinance, which is for cryptocurrency enthusiasts, will result in reprimands from the community administrator in charge of community oversight.

Additionally, you may locate other communities by scrolling below.

Making Your First Hive Post

You should write your introductory article on Hive like a newbie. To do this, make sure your well crafted content and photos adhere to the following rules.

Observe that the introductory post is to be only made once. You don't have to write an introduction post every time you communicate with members of other communities. It's covered in the first.

Rules for the introduction post

You may use these questions as a starting point for creating an excellent introductory article, but don't be afraid to add more, vary, or just go with the flow!

1. Tell me about yourself.

Telling us your username, true name, nick name, and a few other details about yourself will be a huge help. Not all personal information is required to be shared, such as your home address or date of birth, but providing us with your name, origins, and any other information you would want to submit can help us verify that you are who you say you are.

2. What first drew you to cryptocurrency?

If you are interested in cryptocurrencies, please tell us about your interactions with them. Is hive/leofinance your first venture with cryptocurrency? Do you engage in trading? How did you find out about our website?

3. What made you choose to sign up for hive.leofinance.io?

We would be happy to hear about your experience if you came to our platform from a friend recommendation, if you watched a video that encouraged you to join, or if you came across a post on Twitter.

Furthermore, the original "cause" will be very appreciative of a mention.

4. Tell us a little bit more about your ambitions and interests.

What information are you going to share? Do you have a particular passion or pastime that you would like to write about?

5. Photo Share a picture of yourself carrying a piece of paper with the date and your username on it. This is to demonstrate that we are actual people. While posting your own photo is not required, we would appreciate and welcome any unique images you choose to submit. It

6. Avoid overanalyzing!

It is not necessary to overthink. A shorter, more coherent post is preferable to a lengthy one that contains a ton of extraneous content. There will be plenty of possibilities for you to read other people's articles, be inspired, and create a lot of blogs!

7. Don't just publish and go

It's likely that your postings may receive one or more comments. Be sure to return and read them, respond to any questions, and see what other people have to say. Take pleasure in being a part of a robust and cohesive crypto community!

An additional tip

Visit giftgiver.site, https://giftgiver.site/, to receive some delegation for your initial days on the platform. This will assist you with your initial posts, comments, and other activities until you obtain your first earned tokens.

An additional tip 2: Post every day, at least in the initial days. Reward points are awarded seven days after your post, so you'll start getting what you won after that time.

Read chapter three through to the end before creating your first introduction post on Hive.

Chapter 3: Maximizing Content Creation on Hive

Crafting Engaging Content for Hive

Understanding the characteristics of the platform, community preferences, and best practices for producing content that connects with the audience are essential to crafting compelling content for Hive. You will need to define the following in order to craft an engaging content:

Recognizing the Target Audience:

Recognize the expectations, inclinations, and preferences of the Hive community you are aiming for. It's possible that different communities inside Hive have different interests.

Interact with the Community

Take part in conversations, leave comments on other people's postings, and learn what kinds of content get good response.

Producing Captivating Content

- **Authenticity and Originality**: Provide distinct viewpoints, innovative concepts, and genuine contents. Users of Hive value authentic content that offers value. Avoid employing artificial intelligence techniques to create your content.

- **Strong Titles and Introductions**: Grab readers' interest and persuade them to continue reading with attention-grabbing titles and introductions.

  Craft compelling stories that captivate your listeners through storytelling. To establish an emotional connection, share personal tales or observations.

Increasing Interactivity and Value

- **Content for Education**: Offer helpful hints, instructions, or lessons pertaining to your area of expertise. Content that is educational usually does well.

- **Pose Inquiries and Promote Conversations**: Post queries, solicit feedback, and promote conversation to pique readers' interest.

- **Engage & Collaborate**: Take part in projects or conversations in group settings or with other people. Reaching a larger audience is typically the result of interacting with others.

Making Effective Use of Visuals and Multimedia

To enhance your content use images, video, infographics, and high-quality pictures. Visual components frequently increase interest. Verify the photos are yours. Use of copyrighted photos is prohibited. You may also provide a link to one of your own YouTube videos that goes into further detail about your material.

The websites listed below provide free photos for download:

- https://pixabay.com
- https://unsplash.com
- https://pexels.com

It is advisable to cite the image's original source inside your writing.

Organizing and Showcasing Your Content

- **Employ formatting:** Use headers, bullet points, or numbered lists to divide the text into manageable sections. Readability is improved by this.

- **Effective Tag Use**: To classify your content and target the appropriate audience, use pertinent tags. Take note of popular or trending tags in your industry.

A Guideline for Crafting Of Content

I will be creating a post about hive in this part. When creating your content, you must keep the following in mind.

Conditions for creating content

1. Select the appropriate community to promote the content you create in.

2. Choose an appropriate title.

3. Make a draft of your topic with notes or use a word processing program.

4. Make sure the information you write is at least 500 words and above

5. Sort your content into paragraphs.

6. Make any necessary corrections and punctuate correctly.

7. Prepare your photos.

8. Compose your article.

9. Format the information.

Answer your responses.

I'm going to create a little piece of content about *"Becoming the Woman of Your Dreams."*

Following the guidelines:

1. "LadiesofHive" is the appropriate community that endorses such stuff. I was under the impression that you were already a subscriber.

2. Based on the aforementioned prerequisites, "How to Become a Woman of Your Dreams" would be a fitting title for the subject matter.

3. I will compose my text on my word processor, such as Microsoft Office or Notepad.

I am going to write a 200 word guide on how to become the lady of your dreams just for the purpose of this guide.

Greetings of the season to everybody. I hope you are enjoying yourself and your celebrations throughout this festive season. I'm wishing everyone a joyful Christmas and a prosperous new year.

For girls who cross over from childhood to adolescence, the question of how to become the woman of their dreams is a perennial one. In this episode, I'll be discussing the essential conditions that must be met in order to provide a satisfactory response to this question in order to live a happy life.

First and foremost, in today's environment, it is crucial for a woman to find her own voice. What kind of lady are you? What are your life's passions, and how do you plan to pursue them?

Second, establishing objectives based on your life's priorities is crucial. Make a list of the goals you hope to accomplish in the next days and ask yourself what steps you need to take each day to get there.

You can achieve your objectives if you have followed both recommendations and added diligence and frequent prayers.

I sincerely appreciate you visiting my site, and I hope you have an amazing weekend.

Figure 16: Source -- Raycorbett docs

4 -6. Having gone through the entire document to correct for errors.

7. I will proceed to get images that supports my content. You can search for free images on the sites listed above.

8. It time to make the post.

Publishing your Post

I'm going to use the simple hive interface for the sake of this lesson.

Take the actions listed below:

i.   Visit https://hive.blog and make sure you are logged in.

ii. Tap the pencil symbol located on the screen's right side.

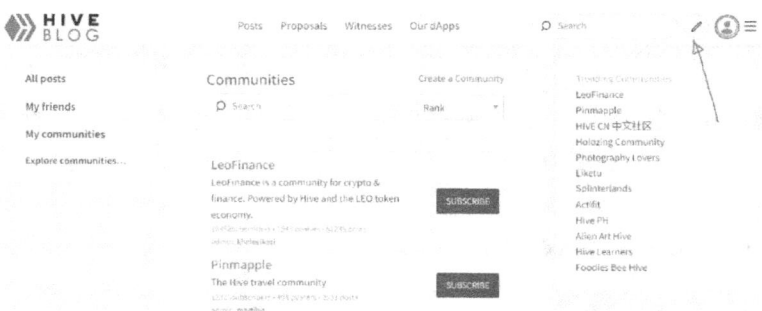

Figure 17: Source --hive.blog

You will be prompted to the interface as seen below.

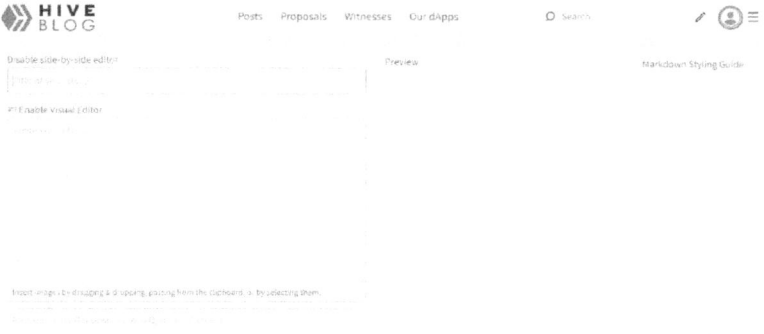

Figure 18: Source--hive.blog

iii. To add your title, copy and paste it in the title field. In the story section, copy and paste what you have written.

The display preview of your material is located on the left side of your screen.

Once you've done so, your content ought to resemble the illustration below. Make sure the paragraphs and spacing are appropriate.

Figure 19: Source--hive.blog

iv. Place the photographs where it is appropriate. To accomplish this, move the pointer to the desired spot and click "selecting them" from the menu that appears beneath your editor.

v. Choose the picture you want to use as the device's wallpaper. The preview portion will display the photographs, while the link will be visible.

vi. We must justify the text using the code below in order to format the information.

* -- should be placed at the beginning of your content*

</div> -- should be placed at the end of your content.

Citing your picture

Copy the URL from the free website where you found your images, then insert it into the link below to reference your image. Copy the template and paste after your image link in the editor.

If Image is yours, use the template below image link

<center> This Image is Mine </center>

If image was gotten from a free website, use

[Source](website link to the image)

vii. You might decide to offer a succinct synopsis of your material.

viii. Add your tags here.

The community name, in our example, "ladiesofhive," should be the first tag you use. Next, use the hashtag for the title of your content, such as "womanofmydreams," and any additional tags that could come after.

To view trending tags used, look through the community's earlier posts.

As a beginner, the name of the community is the first tag you should use when creating an introductory post. Since the OCD community helps and mentors new users on Hive, it makes sense to create your introduction post in OCD. There, you may write an introduction.

You should use #introduceyourself as the following tag and any others that come after. Look through other community members' introductory posts to get ideas on how to organize yours.

ix. Decide which community you want to publish to. The community in this instance is "Ladiesofhive."

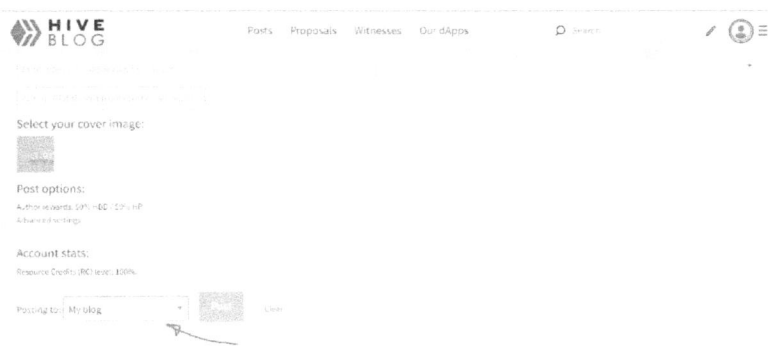

Figure 20: Source--hive.blog

Before you can post anything in the community, you need to be a subscriber.

Click on advanced setting, if you are publishing a post as a beginner set your "Author rewards" to 100% powerup in order to build your influence on the blockchain. To do so, click on advanced settings.

Figure 21: Source--hive.blog

Click on Author rewards and select 100% power up, scroll down and click on save.

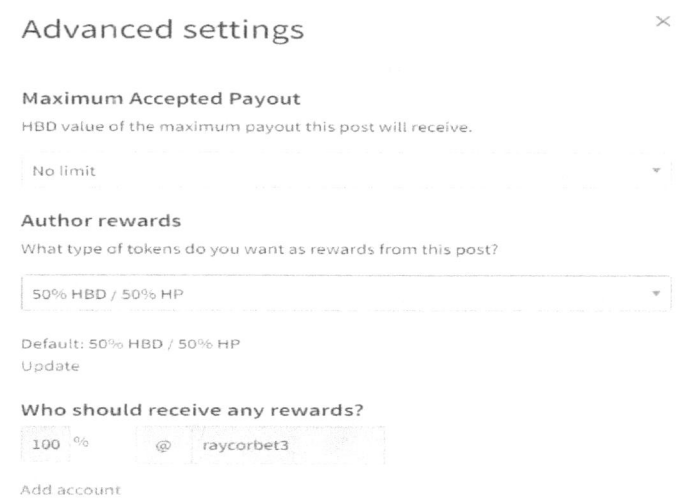

Figure 22: Source--hive.blog

Go through your article once more, Include your video links at appropriate places. If required.

x. Click on post.

Chapter 4: Monetization Strategies on Hive

Understanding Crypto Rewards on Hive

Hive is a dynamic social environment powered by blockchain technology that provides members, curators, and content producers with an exclusive rewards program. Within seven days of the post's publication, any payouts you get automatically show up in your account. All you need to do is use your active private key to log into your wallet.

Understanding these cryptocurrency benefits fundamentally entails exploring the complex incentive systems of the site.

The Hive Reward Scheme

Voting power and hive power (HP)

The idea of Hive Power (HP) is fundamental to the Hive incentive system. Users have the ability to exchange their Hive tokens for HP, which gives them network influence. One may curate content and get prizes more easily the more HP they own.

Voting Power is a measure of a user's capacity to make significant votes. Votes cast by users gradually lose value, which promotes regular use of the platform.

Rewards for Authors and Curators

When content whether articles, photos, or videos gets upvotes, authors are rewarded. These prizes are determined by a number of variables, including as the voter's HP, engagement, and the content's perceived worth.

Conversely, those that find and upvote worthwhile material early on receive curation benefits. By encouraging users to recognize and promote high-quality postings, this promotes a culture of content discovery.

Comprehending the 50/50 Distribution: Writer and curator

Rewards are divided equally between the curators and the author of a post. The platform has changed to a 50/50 distribution scheme, which makes the incentive structure fairer. The user will be able to collect Hive Power and Hive Backed dollar (HBD) following each payout. If you set your rewards to 50% HP and 50% HBD, you can power up again to boost your influence or trade the HBD instantaneously.

Powering Up and Powering Down

Users have the ability to 'Power Up', which increases their influence and possible rewards, by turning their liquid Hive into HP. In contrast, 'Powering Down' enables customers to progressively access their rewards by converting HP back into liquid Hive over time.

Getting the Most Out of Your Content to Make Crypto

Creating content on Hive is about optimizing your chances of earning cryptocurrency rewards, not just about sharing. In order to get the most of this platform, think about utilizing following techniques for content optimization:

1. Excellence Is Essential

On Hive, content quality is king. Original, interesting, and educational content usually receives greater attention and incentives. To fascinate your audience, devote time to research, storytelling, or providing original viewpoints.

2. Attractiveness Is Important

Images convey a lot. Add visually stimulating pictures, infographics, or videos to enhance your textual material. Not only may captivating images improve your content, but they can also increase interaction and bring about benefits.

3. Involve and Communicate

Involving the community is essential. Participate in conversations, answer remarks, and engage with other Hivers. Interacting with others not only helps you build relationships but also makes your material more visible, which might result in bigger benefits.

4. Time and Regularity

Regular posting might have a favorable effect on your awards. Recognize when your audience is most engaged and post during those hours to increase visibility. Providing high-quality material consistently fosters audience growth and continuous support.

5. Employ Applicable Tags

Make use of pertinent tags for precise content classification. Tags make it easier for readers who are interested in particular subjects to find your writings. Choosing the right tags improves your content's exposure in certain communities on Hive.

6. Make Use of Hive Power

To improve your Hive Power (HP), power up your Hive tokens. Higher potential benefits and greater influence are correlated with higher HP. Additionally, think about upvoting other people's great material to curate it yourself and receive rewards for your efforts.

7. Promote Involvement

Prompts with a call to action (CTA) can boost participation. Post queries, requests for feedback, or start conversations in your postings. In addition to adding value to your material, encouraging reader interaction also raises the possibility of incentives.

Examining the Token Ecosystem of Hive

The world of Hive's token ecosystem is broad and complex, encompassing more than just the native HIVE token. To gain an understanding of this ecosystem, one must investigate the many tokens that support the operation and liveliness of the platform.

1. The HIVE Token

HIVE is the platform's primary token and is essential. It powers the network's operations, facilitates communication, and provides incentives for the development and curation of information.

Users can use it to reward other users in the ecosystem, trade, or power up (convert to Hive Power).

2. Hive Power (HP)

A user's impact on the platform is represented by their Hive Power. Users get more substantial voting power when HIVE is converted to Hive Power, which enables them to curate material and receive more curation benefits. A user's votes have more weight the more HP they possess.

3. HBD (Hive Backed Dollars)

A stablecoin linked to the US dollar is called HBD. Through the platform's internal market, users may convert their HIVE to HBD, offering stability in the face of volatility in the cryptocurrency market. It serves as a platform for users to manage their money and reduce risk inside the Hive ecosystem.

4. Hive Engine Tokens

Based on Hive, Hive Engine is a decentralized smart contract platform. It offers a variety of tokens, each with a special function and use case. These tokens, which range from community-specific tokens to gaming tokens, enhance the Hive ecosystem by supporting a variety of uses and features.

Tokens from the Hive Engine Examples

LEO: A token used mostly on the LeoFinance platform, linked to the Hive financial and investing community.

STEM: Providing resources for scientific, technology, engineering, and math content, STEM encourages the production of new content and participation in these fields.

CTP: The ClickTrackProfit community is supported by the CTP token, which promotes interaction with material connected to online business and marketing.

5. Additional Community Coins

Several Hive communities have unveiled their own tokens in addition to Hive Engine tokens. Within their various communities, these tokens frequently have defined functions that encourage participation in the community, honor contributions, or support certain initiatives.

Chapter 5: Growing Your Audience and Community

Building a Following on Hive

Developing a devoted fan base on Hive requires a combination of interaction, regularity, high-caliber content production, and community involvement. This is a how-to tutorial for gaining and keeping followers:

1. Reliable, High-Quality Content

Maintaining consistency is essential. Share interesting, well-written material on a regular basis that connects with your audience. Whether you publish comments, videos, photographs, or articles, having a regular posting schedule keeps your audience interested and returning back for more.

2. Involvement Is Essential

Talk to your listeners and other Hivers. Participate in conversations, answer comments on your posts, and engage authentically with the material of others. Developing connections makes people feel like they are a part of the community and motivates them to support and follow your work.

3. Make Good Use of Tags

To organize and make your material more visible, use pertinent tags. Select tags that appropriately describe your material and correspond with your target audience's interests. This makes it easier for your posts to be seen by the appropriate Hive community members.

4. Connect and Work Together

Work together with other artists and people of the community. Participating in group projects, teamwork, or showcasing other users' material can help you expand your following and reach on the network.

5. Provide Diversity and Value

To appeal to a wide range of interests, diversify your material. Offer informational articles, amusement, insider knowledge, or specialized knowledge. Providing a variety of information can help you maintain the interest of your followers and appeal to a wider audience.

6. Boost the Visibility of Your Hive

Advertise your Hive presence on other websites and social media networks. Users from other platforms might be drawn to your Hive profile for more captivating material by sharing excerpts or trailers of your work.

7. Utilize Communities of Hive

Participate fully in Hive communities that are pertinent to the information you write. Communities act as gathering places for others who share your interests, giving you the chance to interact with a more narrow or topic-focused audience.

8. Add Value Through Communication

Organize prizes, competitions, or conversations that inspire user involvement. By fostering a feeling of community engagement, providing value beyond your normal material will help you draw in new followers and hold onto your current ones.

Chapter 6: Advanced Hive Techniques

Powering Up

In order to power up on Hive, you must convert your Hive tokens into Hive Power (HP). This process increases your influence on the platform and opens up a number of advantages, such as more voting power and possible prizes. Your hive power grows as you power up.

Within the Hive ecosystem, a user's vested interest and power are represented by their Hive Power. Users cannot instantly withdraw their HP after Power Up, which turns their liquid Hive tokens into HP. This procedure aids in:

Increasing the Sway of Votes: Increased HP results in increased voting power, giving people the ability to make more meaningful votes on material they value.

Improving Reward Structure: The potential incentives for engaging in the platform and curating content rise with the amount of HP held.

Ways to power up.

You need to have some liquid hive assets or hive-backed dollars in your wallet in order to power up.

Get to Your Wallet: Go to your Hive wallet by clicking the drop-down hive icon on the platform.

Figure 23: Source--hive.blog

2. Select Power Up: From the wallet interface, choose the Power Up option.

3. Enter Amount: Indicate the quantity of e-wallets you want to exchange for hive power.

4. Confirm Transaction: Go over the information and make sure the Power Up transaction is correct.

Advantages of Increasing Influence

Having more HP enables you to support and influence the visibility of material you believe in by giving your votes greater weight.

Curation incentives: When you upvote worthwhile material, Powering Up entitles you to more curation incentives.

Supporting the Network: Users help the Hive network remain stable and expand, which bolsters the network's resilience and sustainability.

Powering Down

If a user chooses to Power Down, HP will gradually be converted back into liquid Hive tokens over a predetermined amount of time. With this feature, one may manage their holdings more freely and yet reap the rewards of more influence during the Power Up phase.

To power down,

1. Click on the downward arrow on Hive Power section.

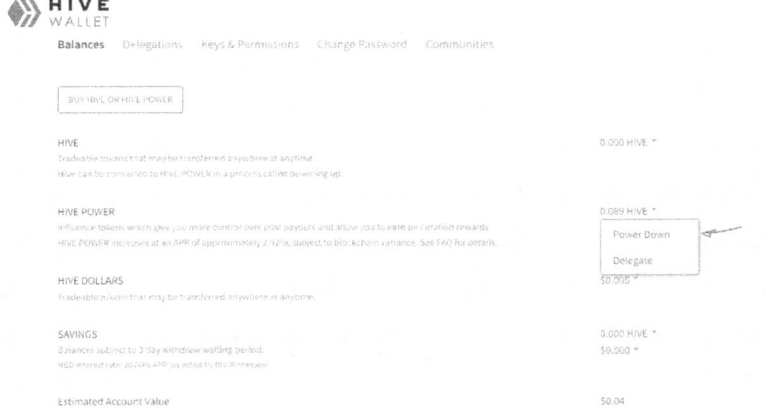

Figure 24: Source--hive.blog

2. Select power down.

3. Enter the amount of Liquid Hive you want to powerdown and click on power down button.

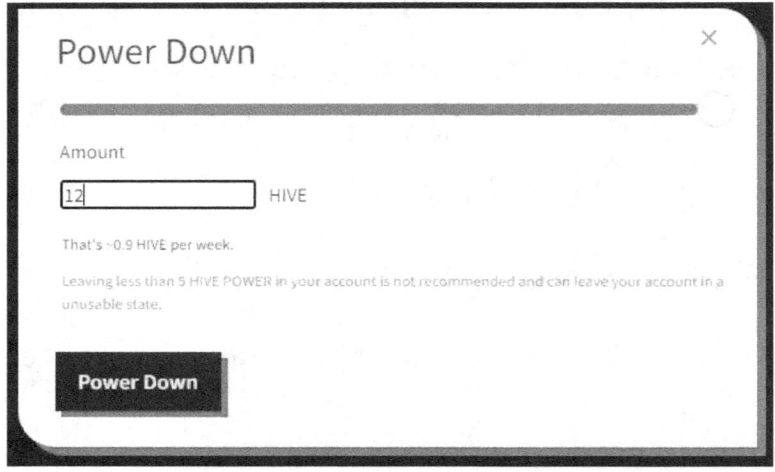

Figure 25: Source--hive.blog

Converting Your HBD to HIVE

Based on your payout preferences, rewards are divided into 50% HBD and 50% HP. In order to convert your HBD into HIVE which can be utilized for a variety of things, such trading on different platforms.

Follow the guidelines

1. Navigate to your wallet, log in with your active key and username.

2. Click the drop-down arrow and choose market under the Hive Dollars section.

Figure 26: Source--hive.blog

The interface is similar as seen below.

Figure 27: Source--hive.blog

By converting your HBD to Hive, you are essentially using your HBD to purchase Hive. The area on the left that says "buy Hive" is what we'll be using. If you wish to sell your hive, follow suit.

3. After entering the quantity of HBD you want to exchange for hive, the appropriate hive amount is shown.

HIVE WALLET

BUY HIVE

SELL HIVE

PRICE	0.351131	HBD/HIVE
AMOUNT	0.015	HIVE
TOTAL	0.005	HBD (\$)

PRICE	0.351310	HBD/HIVE
AMOUNT		HIVE
TOTAL		HBD (\$)

Buy Orders

Total HBD (\$)	HBD (\$)	Hive	Price
18.246	18.246	29.190	0.351130
18.695	4.350	23.873	0.350144
22.695	2.000	5.712	0.350140
42.695	20.000	57.126	0.350048
240.695	200.000	571.359	0.350042
244.197	3.502	10.034	0.349013
244.665	0.636	2.800	0.349000
247.374	2.569	7.362	0.348854

Sell Orders

Price	Hive	HBD (\$)
0.351290	10.117	3.554
0.351954	69.333	24.402
0.351936	5.549	1.953
0.352090	125.738	44.271
0.352396	10350.410	3650.611
0.358118	32.490	11.541
0.353437	56.585	19.990
0.353442	565.864	200.000

Trade History

Total HBD (\$)	Date	Price	Hive	HBD (\$)
3.554	4 minutes ago	0.351609	5.695	1.998
27.956	6 minutes ago	0.351167	1.028	0.361
29.909	7 minutes ago	0.352571	0.136	0.125
74.180	7 minutes ago	0.352154	0.673	0.237
3724.791	10 minutes ago	0.350241	46.702	16.357
3736.232	10 minutes ago	0.350282	6.710	2.001
3756.232	10 minutes ago	0.350018	57.194	20.000
3956.232	10 minutes ago	0.349101	572.930	200.000

Figure 28: Source--hive.blog

4. Select "Buy Hive."

Your deal will be matched with a buyer who is accessible via the blockchain algorithm.

You just need to wait a little while for the Hive to instantly appear in your wallet.

Chapter 7: Navigating Challenges and Solutions

Overcoming Common Hurdles on Hive

Like any thriving online community, navigating the Hive platform has some hurdles. In order to get the most out of the platform and reach your full potential, you must overcome these obstacles. The following are typical challenges users encounter on Hive, along with solutions:

1. **Content Being Visible**: When their content gets lost in a flood of posts, new users frequently struggle to get it recognized.

   The solution is efficient tagging. To better organize your information and make it more visible among the groups you want to reach, use pertinent tags.

- **Engagement**: Give intelligent comments on other users' content to engage them. Your profile and posts may get more attention if you participate in meaningful ways.

2. **Building an Audience**: Especially for newbies, gaining followers and cultivating a devoted following can be difficult.

   Consistency and quality are the solution. Post excellent stuff frequently to draw and keep followers.

▪ **Engagement**: Engage your audience by leaving comments and starting conversations. Developing connections helps you attract devoted followers.

3. **The Difficulty of Understanding Rewards and Voting**: It might be difficult to comprehend the intricate voting dynamics and reward systems.

   Research and Learning as a Solution Spend some time learning about how Hive Power, curation, and incentives operate. Participate in community guides, tutorials, and other user interactions to expand your expertise.

- **Experimentation:** To understand how incentives are allocated, start small and try voting, Powering Up, and interacting with content.

4. **Maintaining Consistency Difficulty**: Creating high-quality material on a regular basis may be taxing and might eventually result in fatigue.

Resolution:

- **Planning Content**: To be consistent without going crazy, prepare your content in advance.
- **Take pauses**: In order to prevent burnout, it is essential to take pauses as needed. Consistency refers to a steady, sustainable pace rather than constant output.

Chapter 8: Legal Aspects

Maintaining Order in the Hive Space

In addition to following the platform's rules, staying compliant in the Hive environment entails keeping in mind larger legal and moral issues that are pertinent to online communities and blockchain-based platforms. Here are some important things to think about:

1. Guidelines for the Platform

- **Conditions of Service**: Read the Hive terms of service, which include guidelines for appropriate conduct, acceptable material, and forbidden actions.

- **Community Rules and Guidelines**: Hive communities may each have their own set of rules and regulations. When interacting with such cultures, respect and adherence to these standards are expected.

2. Adherence to the Law

- **Copyright and Intellectual Property**: Be mindful of your rights to intellectual property. Refrain from using content protected by copyright without permission or acknowledgement.

- **Legal Compliance:** Make sure that the content you create and the things you do on Hive abide by all applicable national and international laws, especially those pertaining to finance and data protection.

3. Moral Aspects

- **Openness**: Be open and honest in all that you do, particularly when it comes to voting, curation, and financial incentives.
- **Behaving with Respect**: Even when there are arguments or differences, always act with civility and constructiveness.

- **Steer clear of Plagiarism**: When utilizing someone else's work or citing outside sources, do not copy and make sure to provide correct credit. Refrain from publishing content from another user's website on another platform for your hive. You'll face harsh consequences.

4. Privacy and Security

- **Safeguarding Personal Data**: Be considerate of others' privacy and refrain from disclosing private data without authorization.

- **Security Procedures**: Make sure your Hive account is secure by setting up the required security measures and using strong passwords.

5. Policies against Abuse and Spam

- **Steer clear of spam**: Avoid sending unsolicited messages or taking part in activities that the community can interpret as spam.
- **Report any abuse**: Inform the proper Hive community administrators of any abusive conduct, spam, or platform policy breaches.

6. Ongoing Education and Adjustment

- **Remain Up to Date:** Stay informed about any modifications to community standards, legal requirements, and platform regulations.

- **Adaptation**: Keep an open mind to changing your conduct in response to criticism, changing community norms, and platform upgrades.

Extra Bonus

I want to express my sincere appreciation to each and every one of the incredible readers who have bought my book. It means the world to me that you choose to buy my stuff and interact with it. Your encouragement inspires me to continue producing and offering this amazing community insightful content.

As a thank you, allow me to introduce you to a wonderful resource that can help you write better, particularly if you're trying to get better at grammar and sentence construction.

Presenting Quilbot: Your Enhancing Grammar Paraphrasing Tool

Although writing is a lovely art, it's not always simple to express our ideas clearly. Here comes Quilbot, an effective paraphrase tool that helps people improve their writing by rearranging phrases, correcting syntax, and making their work easier to read.

Quilbot For What Reason?

Efficient Paraphrasing: Quilbot reduces complicated statements to a simpler form without changing the meaning of the original sentence.

Grammar Enhancement: It helps those who have trouble with grammar by offering suggestions for sentence structure and fixes.

Time-saving Solution: You may ensure clarity and coherence in your material quickly by speeding up the writing process using Quilbot.

How Quilbot Operates

Text input: To use Quilbot, just type your words into its interface.

Paraphrase and Improve: Quilbot evaluates your work, generates paraphrases, and makes recommendations for better syntax and legibility.

Refine and Perfect: Go over the recommendations, pick the enhancements that work best for your writing style, and easily refine your article.

Whether you're an experienced writer looking for improvement or someone who wants to communicate more clearly, Quilbot is a trustworthy partner on your writing path. Its extensive paraphrase capabilities and easy-to-use design make it a priceless resource for writers who want to improve their skills.

Here is the link to access quilbot below

Link https://quilbot.com

References

http://inleo.io/@katerinaramm/7-tips-to-assist-you-in-writing-your-first-introduction-post-for-leofinance-hive

To My Honored Audience

Thank you very much for your recommendations! Once you have read my work, kindly take a moment to leave a review. Your advice aids in my writing growth. Thank you very much.

www.ingramcontent.com/pod-product-compliance
Lightning Source LLC
Chambersburg PA
CBHW062354290526
45794CB00005B/2216